1½

Women

In

Science

AVA REID

Content

Prologue 5

Ada Lovelace, The Girl Who Saw the Future 8

Marie Curie, The Woman Who Made Stones Glow 17

Jane Goodall, The Girl Who Talked to Chimpanzees 25

Mae Jemison, Doctor Among the Stars 33

Tu Youyou, the Malaria Maverick 41

Sylvia Earle, The Mermaid Scientist 47

Hedy Lamarr, The Movie Star Inventor 53

Grace Hopper, The Code Whisperer 59

Katherine Johnson, The Rocket Mathematician 66

Rosalind Franklin, The Photo that Changed the World 72

Elizabeth Blackwell, The Brave Doctor 78

Chien-Shiung Wu, The Queen of the Experiment 86

Prologue

The pages of history are filled with tales of explorers and visionaries, scientists and revolutionaries. For centuries, these stories have often been dominated by men - courageous inventors, and pioneering thinkers, whose names have echoed across generations. And while their achievements are indeed worthy of our admiration, there are other stories, equally remarkable, that have long lingered in the shadows.

This is a book about women. Brilliant women. Determined women. Women who dared to think differently, to challenge expectations, and to make groundbreaking discoveries that changed the very fabric of our world. From counting stars to cracking codes, from battling disease to defying physics, they refused to accept a world that said "you can't" simply because they were born female.

Their paths were not always easy. They faced closed doors, dismissive colleagues, and a world steeped in the prejudice that genius had only one gender. Yet they persevered, fueled by an insatiable curiosity and a belief in the boundless possibilities that lay on the other side of the *impossible*.

Within these pages, you will meet a mathematician whose calculations paved the way to the moon, a biologist who whispered secrets to chimpanzees, a doctor who refused to stand idly by while others suffered. Alongside them are codebreakers, inventors, physicists, and countless women whose discoveries pushed the boundaries of what we know and who we are.

This book is a celebration of their intellect, their determination, and their profound impact on our world. But most of all, it's an invitation. An invitation to look beyond the obvious, to seek out the unsung heroes, the hidden brilliance that resides in every generation. For if these women could transform the world with the power of their minds, imagine the possibilities that lie within us all.

Ada Lovelace, The Girl Who Saw the Future

In the heart of 19th-century London, an era of horse-drawn carriages and flickering gas lamps, a young girl named Ada Lovelace possessed a mind that crackled with the electricity of the future. While her world prized poetry and fine stitching, Ada found her own unique poetry in the patterns of mathematics and the intricate dance of logic. She was a pioneer, a visionary - a brilliant mind born far too early for her world to fully understand.

Ada Augusta Byron was born in 1815, the only legitimate child of the celebrated and tempestuous poet Lord Byron. It was a scandalous match from the start - her father the darling of society with his passionate verse, her mother a strict, mathematically-minded woman nicknamed "The Princess of Parallelograms" by her less-than-fond husband. The marriage was tumultuous, and short-lived.

Baby Ada would never truly know her famous father. Lord Byron left England shortly after her birth, embarking on travels that fueled his poetry, but leaving a void in his daughter's life. Ada clung to the idea of her brilliant but absent father, her own wild imagination perhaps finding an echo in his rebellious spirit.

Her mother, Lady Anne Isabella Byron, was determined that her daughter would not follow her father's path of what she considered frivolous emotions and reckless impulses. She would raise Ada to be rational, logical, grounded in the unyielding power of mathematics. To that end, she hired tutors for Ada in science and mathematics, subjects rarely taught to girls in that era, and made sure her daughter was drilled in the precision of numbers.

This might seem a harsh way to counterbalance her absent father's influence, but it ignited a spark in Ada. She took to logic the way other children took to nursery rhymes. The world became a puzzle to be picked apart, its workings revealed through the application of reason. Yet, within her deeply analytical mind lived a vibrant imagination - a touch of her father's legacy, perhaps. It was a combination that would set her apart and propel her on a path unlike any woman of her time.

Ada wasn't a robust child, and her childhood was punctuated by bouts of illness. But confined to bedrest, she found solace in the world of numbers. Her mother, sensing this could turn into a passion, provided her with puzzles and challenges to exercise her mind. Here, in a house where poetry and passion reigned, a different kind of artistry was being born.

From a young age, Ada was drawn to machines. She meticulously took apart toys to understand how their springs and levers worked. She designed fantastical inventions, once even trying to create a workable flying machine fueled by steam. Numbers swirled in her mind, creating patterns and possibilities she was eager to unleash on the world.

Then, a change of fortune would lead her to a discovery that would change the course of her life. Her mother, through social connections, secured an invitation for them both to a party hosted by the renowned inventor and mathematician Charles Babbage. It was here that twelve-year-old Ada first laid eyes on a machine that would ignite her imagination - the Difference Engine.

The Difference Engine was a marvel of engineering for its time. A room-sized behemoth of polished brass gears, cogs, and levers, it could calculate and print complex mathematical tables, a task both tedious and error-prone for humans to complete. While most guests were merely impressed by the machine's imposing presence, Ada was captivated.

She peppered Mr. Babbage with questions, her young mind leaping far beyond simple calculations. She saw that this machine, marvelous as it was, represented something far greater. If numbers could be used to give instructions to a mechanical device to do calculations, then could they be used to instruct machines to do other complex tasks?

Babbage, a man used to being humored more than understood, was taken aback by the young Ada's insight. He recognized a kindred spirit, a mind that could think in the structured, precise way his own inventions demanded. From that day on, a mentorship and a friendship blossomed, one that would unlock Ada's extraordinary potential and propel her on a path few dared to imagine.

Babbage became Ada's guide into the evolving world of mathematics and invention. But their collaboration would reach far beyond mere calculations. In the Difference Engine's successor, the unbuilt Analytical Engine, they saw a machine that was not merely a calculator, but something truly revolutionary.

The Analytical Engine, though never fully constructed in Ada's lifetime, held the potential to be programmed with instructions to perform complex tasks - the precursor of modern computers. It was meant to use punchcards, similar to how early looms were programmed to weave intricate patterns, but instead of patterns in cloth, this machine would manipulate numbers and symbols.

Ada, with her extraordinary mind, understood the true power of this machine. She realized that numbers could be used to represent more than just quantities. They could represent letters, musical notes, even the complex code of logic itself. With the right instructions, the machine could not just calculate, but also compose music, create images, or even play games. This was a radical leap, and most people simply couldn't grasp the concept.

This was where Ada Lovelace's genius shone through. She began writing instructions, or programs, for the Analytical Engine. These programs weren't merely dry calculations; they were the first algorithms for a computer that didn't yet exist. She became the world's first computer programmer - a century before the first electronic computer blinked into existence.

Ada translated a complex mathematical paper about the Analytical Engine from French to English. But crucially, she added extensive notes of her own that went far beyond mere translation. It was within these notes that she outlined the machine's true potential and the intricate programs she envisioned for it.

Ada wrote of the machine one day creating complex music, of generating graphics, and the practical uses it might have for both science and industry. These weren't flights of fancy, but insights based on her deep understanding of how the interplay of mathematics and logic could direct a machine. Sadly, the technology of the time limited the full realization of her visions, yet the foundation of computer science had been laid.

Her work was groundbreaking yet met with resistance in a world that saw science as the domain of men. Some dismissed her as Lord Byron's eccentric daughter. Her own health would hold her back, as she battled bouts of illness throughout her short life.

Despite these barriers, Ada's brilliance could not be denied. Though formal university education was closed to her purely because she was a woman, her drive for knowledge never wavered. A woman of both science and society, she was known for her intellect, her wit, and even her connections to the fashionable circles of her day. But beneath the social demands, her mind continued to explore, to analyze, to push the limits of possibility.

Alas, Ada Lovelace's life was tragically cut short. She died in 1852 at the age of 36, succumbing to cancer after a long illness. It would take a century before the true importance of her work was fully recognized. With the advent of electronic computers, scientists rediscovered her writings and were stunned by the foresight of this brilliant woman who imagined the digital age long before the technology to enable it existed.

Ada Lovelace, with her passion for mathematics and her extraordinary imagination, became known as the "Enchantress of Numbers". More importantly, she taught us that the greatest innovations are often those born in minds that see the world differently. Today, she is celebrated as a pioneer of computer science, an inspiration to everyone, especially girls, who dream of changing the world through the power of ideas.

Marie Curie, The Woman Who Made Stones Glow

In the bustling city of Warsaw, nestled within the heart of Poland, a young girl named Maria Skłodowska possessed a relentless curiosity that shimmered brighter than the city lights. Her eyes held a determined glint as she examined the world, not only seeing what was there, but questioning what might be hidden.

Maria, or Manya as her family called her, was born into an era when opportunities for women, especially those drawn to science, were as scarce as gold dust. In a time when girls were expected to learn needlework and dream of becoming wives, Manya dreamt of laboratories and the mysteries concealed within the universe.

Her parents, both dedicated teachers, nurtured their daughter's inquisitive nature. Her father instilled a love for physics and mathematics, while her mother carefully tended to their home despite years of ill health. Their modest house overflowed with books, makeshift science tools, and a spirit of learning that formed the bedrock of Maria's childhood.

But tragedy cast a long shadow over the Skłodowska household. Loss and hardship visited their family, shaking young Maria's world. Yet, through the heartache, a quiet strength took root within her. Where others might have crumbled, Maria resolved to make something of her life, to honor those she'd lost with the unwavering pursuit of knowledge.

Maria excelled in school, her mind leaping over problems that baffled her classmates. But her homeland, Poland, was under the oppressive rule of Russia, and universities barred women from attending. Maria made a pact with her beloved older sister, Bronya: she would work as a governess, supporting Bronya's education in medicine in Paris. Afterward, Bronya would return the favor, helping Maria achieve her own university dreams.

And so, Maria endured long, hard years of work, saving every penny for a future she could only imagine. Finally, her moment came. Leaving behind her cherished family, she boarded a train bound for Paris, her heart pounding with both excitement and a healthy dose of fear.

In the City of Lights, Maria shed her Polish name, becoming 'Marie'. She enrolled at the prestigious Sorbonne University, immersing herself in the study of physics and mathematics. Life was far from easy. She lived in a meager little attic, often surviving on nothing but bread and tea to save precious funds for tuition. But Marie was driven by a fire that no hardship could quench. She studied with unwavering focus, her determination making up for any lack of comforts.

Marie not only excelled, she thrived. She graduated at the top of her class, a feat made even more remarkable as a woman in a male-dominated field. Eager to continue her exploration of the scientific world, Marie embarked on a new project, investigating a strange phenomenon in certain minerals. Some, like uranium, seemed to emit invisible rays that could fog photographic plates, even without exposure to light. The cause was a mystery that called to her like a siren's song.

It was within a humble laboratory, more like a drafty shed than a place of scientific breakthroughs, that Marie began her groundbreaking work. Here, she met a fellow brilliant scientist, Pierre Curie. A quiet, thoughtful man, Pierre shared Marie's passion for untangling the secrets of the universe. They fell in love, their partnership extending far beyond the tender affections of marriage and into the realm of scientific discovery.

Together, Marie and Pierre meticulously studied the mysterious rays emitted by uranium. They experimented endlessly, tracking the intensity of the rays with instruments of Pierre's invention. Marie's intuition told her there was more to the story, that other elements might possess this unusual property.

Following this hunch, Marie tested various minerals. One, called pitchblende, proved to be surprisingly radioactive, far more so than uranium itself. Marie, with unyielding determination, theorized that there must be an undiscovered element hidden within the pitchblende - an element far more powerful than anything known to science.

The search for this elusive element became their all-consuming mission. Obtaining pitchblende was difficult and expensive. The Curies toiled in their makeshift laboratory under the most primitive of conditions. They processed vast quantities of pitchblende, stirring vats of bubbling chemicals in a process both laborious and dangerous.

Yet, their dedication began to bear fruit. In 1898, they announced the discovery of a new, highly radioactive element. Marie, in honor of her beloved homeland, named it polonium. But their work was far from over. That same year, the Curies detected traces of yet another mysterious element within the pitchblende, one that seemed even more powerfully radioactive. They named it radium, for the Latin word for 'ray'.

Isolating pure radium proved to be a monumental task. The Curies processed tons of pitchblende residue, hauling heavy buckets, breathing in noxious fumes, their bodies unknowingly exposed to the harmful radiation they were investigating. Despite the risks and the physically exhausting work, Marie refused to give up. She sensed they were on the cusp of something that would redefine our understanding of the world.

Finally, after years of painstaking labor, Marie Curie isolated a pure sample of radium - a mere speck of a glowing substance that pulsed with an extraordinary energy. Her discovery revolutionized the field of physics. The mysterious rays that had so captivated her were unveiled as the result of atoms decaying, a process that released tremendous bursts of energy. This overthrew the long-held belief that atoms were indivisible.

In 1903, Marie Curie, along with Pierre Curie and another physicist, Henri Becquerel, were awarded the Nobel Prize in Physics for their groundbreaking work on radioactivity. Marie became the first woman to ever receive this prestigious honor.

Yet, triumph was tinged with heartbreak. In 1906, a tragic accident took the life of her beloved Pierre. Marie was devastated, but her will to continue her science never faltered. Shouldering the profound loss, she threw herself back into her work. She took over Pierre's teaching position at the Sorbonne, becoming the first female professor at the university.

In 1911, Marie Curie made history once again, becoming the first, and to this day the only, person to win a Nobel Prize in two different scientific fields. This time, she was awarded the Nobel Prize in Chemistry for her discovery of radium and polonium, and her relentless investigation into their properties.

Marie's discovery of radioactivity had far-reaching implications. It paved the way for revolutionary cancer treatments and offered a powerful tool for peering inside the human body with X-rays. But war cast its gruesome shadow, and Marie recognized the urgent need for portable X-ray machines on the battlefield. Undeterred by the male-dominated field of military medicine, she designed mobile radiology units and even taught herself to drive so she could transport these "Little Curies" to the front lines.

Marie's legacy extends far beyond her groundbreaking discoveries. She became a symbol for women in science, shattering the glass ceiling with her unwavering brilliance and unstoppable determination. Though long overlooked, the dangers of radioactivity became tragically clear when Marie Curie passed away in 1934, from a disease likely caused by her years of exposure.

The woman who made stones glow left an enduring light upon the world - a testament to the extraordinary things that can be achieved through an unyielding curiosity and a spirit that refuses to be confined.

Jane Goodall, The Girl Who Talked to Chimpanzees

From the bustling streets of London to the heart of Africa's untamed wilderness, a young woman named Jane embarked on a journey that would change our understanding of the animal kingdom - and ultimately, ourselves. It was a journey fueled by an unquenchable love for animals, a thirst for knowledge, and a spirit as wild as the creatures she longed to study.

Jane Goodall's story began in bustling London. From her earliest years, Jane displayed an uncanny connection with the natural world. While other children played with dolls, Jane delighted in observing earthworms and befriending neighborhood pets. Her mother, Vanne, fostered her daughter's unusual passion, nurturing her curiosity with gentle encouragement and shelves overflowing with books about animals. A beloved stuffed chimpanzee named Jubilee sparked a particular fascination within Jane, igniting a dream that would one day lead her far from familiar city life.

As a little girl, Jane devoured tales of Tarzan and Doctor Dolittle, her fantasies filled with lush jungles and exotic creatures. She longed to live amongst animals in Africa, a world seemingly so distant from the neat rows of houses and cobbled streets that defined her childhood.

Unlike many girls of the time, Jane's parents never scoffed at her unconventional ambitions. They recognized a spark within their daughter that deserved to be kindled. When the opportunity arose for Jane to leave her job as a secretary and travel to Kenya, both mother and daughter were excited, sensing the transformative power of the adventure to come.

In Kenya, a chance encounter with the famed paleoanthropologist and archaeologist, Dr. Louis Leakey, changed the course of Jane's life. Dr. Leakey recognized a kindred spirit in Jane—a patient observer, a fearless soul drawn to the secrets of the natural world. Although Jane lacked a traditional university education, her boundless enthusiasm and deep love for animals were assets too rare to pass up.

Dr. Leakey held the controversial belief that studying our closest primate relatives, the chimpanzees, could unlock clues about our own evolutionary past. He needed someone daring and dedicated to venture into the wild and observe these intelligent creatures in their natural habitat. Jane, with stars in her eyes, leapt at the opportunity.

And so, in 1960, armed with little more than a notebook, binoculars, and an unwavering determination, Jane ventured into the Gombe Stream Reserve in Tanzania. Her mission: to immerse herself in the world of chimpanzees, a quest that would test her patience, courage, and forever change how we view the boundary between humans and animals.

The early days were filled with frustration. The chimps, unaccustomed to humans, were elusive and wary. They darted through the dense forest, their presence no more than fleeting shadows and distant calls. Jane, however, refused to give up. She spent countless hours trekking through the undergrowth, scrambling up steep slopes, and enduring sweltering heat, all for the possibility of a glimpse into their world.

Slowly, with quiet perseverance, Jane earned the trust of these magnificent creatures. She learned to mimic their calls and observed their behaviors with the utmost respect, careful never to interfere in their natural way of life. She discovered that like humans, chimpanzees were complex individuals with rich social structures and a fascinating array of emotions.

Jane's most groundbreaking discovery came with her observation of chimpanzees making and using tools, a behavior thought to be exclusive to humans. She witnessed them carefully stripping leaves from twigs and using them to fish for termites - a practice requiring both foresight and dexterity. This remarkable find sent shockwaves through the scientific community, challenging the age-old assumption of a clear divide between humans and the rest of the animal kingdom.

In the tradition of giving her study subjects names rather than impersonal numbers, Jane brought the chimpanzees of Gombe to life. There was David Greybeard, the first chimp to truly trust Jane, allowing her closer than ever before. There was the mischievous young Fifi, and the powerful alpha, Mike. Jane's detailed observations revealed their distinct personalities, their family dramas, and their struggle for dominance - a world both strangely familiar and utterly unique.

Jane's commitment to understanding chimpanzees went far beyond scientific curiosity. She witnessed not only their intelligence and capacity for affection, but also their darker side - territory wars, violence, and aggression. Her discoveries painted a complex picture that both celebrated the similarities between humans and chimpanzees, while also reminding us of the delicate balance of our own nature.

As years turned into decades, Jane's work in Gombe evolved. Recognizing the threats facing chimpanzees from deforestation and poaching, she became a powerful advocate for conservation. The Jane Goodall Institute, founded in 1977, continues her legacy, working to protect chimpanzees and their habitats, while promoting a more sustainable and compassionate relationship between humans, animals, and the environment.

Jane's extraordinary journey also transformed her own life. In the heart of the African wilderness, she found a deep sense of belonging. She met and married wildlife photographer Hugo van Lawick, and together they raised a son, affectionately known as 'Grub'. Her time in Gombe, surrounded by nature, was a constant source of both serenity and inspiration.

Jane Goodall's impact extends far beyond the rainforests of Africa. From a shy English girl enchanted by a stuffed chimpanzee to a groundbreaking scientist and global advocate, Jane taught us to question old assumptions and to treat all living creatures with empathy and respect. She showed the world the power of one person's boundless curiosity, determination, and love to truly make a difference.

In bustling classrooms and quiet libraries, young children with a love for animals find inspiration in Jane's remarkable story. They see proof that dreams, however ambitious, can bloom into a reality that changes the world. Because if a girl with a love for animals could transform our understanding of chimpanzees, and therefore ourselves, what extraordinary discoveries might they reveal?

Mae Jemison, Doctor Among the Stars

From a young age, Mae Jemison's eyes were fixed on the heavens. She filled notebooks with sketches of rockets and distant planets, her imagination soaring beyond the boundaries of her small-town life. She longed not only to explore the cosmos, but to leave her own footprints on that vast, starry expanse.

Mae's journey to the stars began in Decatur, Alabama, and later Chicago, Illinois. Born in 1956, Mae grew up in a time of both great change and persistent barriers. The Civil Rights Movement was in full swing, challenging segregation and fighting for equality. While the world around her grappled with these growing pains, Mae found focus and possibility in science and space.

She excelled in school, devouring books on astronomy, physics, and anything that brought the universe a little closer. Her parents, Charlie and Dorothy Jemison, recognized and wholeheartedly supported their daughter's unconventional dreams. Her father, a roofer and carpenter, shared Mae's deep fascination with science, while her mother, a teacher, instilled in her an unyielding belief in her own potential. They filled their home with tools for exploration - telescopes, microscopes, and a sense that the world, as immense as it seemed, was hers for the taking.

Mae's childhood was a whirlwind of interests. She wasn't just drawn to the stars, but to the power of the human body and the vibrant artistry of the world around her. An accomplished dancer, she even considered pursuing a career in dance. But the pull of space remained irresistible. Her heroes weren't just dancers or writers, but the groundbreaking astronauts venturing into the unknown. Watching the Apollo moon landings ignited something within her - a spark of determination that would propel her towards the impossible.

Star Trek offered further inspiration. The character Lieutenant Uhura, a brilliant and capable Black woman on the bridge of a starship, showed Mae that her place was among the pioneers pushing the boundaries of human knowledge and exploration.

But the path to the stars was far from clear. Being a woman, especially a Black woman, in the field of space exploration was an endeavor few had dared attempt. Yet, Mae was undeterred, her resolve as strong as the force of a rocket leaving Earth's atmosphere.

With unwavering focus, Mae attended Stanford University on scholarship, graduating with degrees in both chemical engineering and African American Studies. Refusing to be confined to a single field, Mae believed that the path to innovation required a rich tapestry of knowledge and an understanding of the world from multiple perspectives.

True to her multifaceted passions, she then enrolled in Cornell Medical College, becoming a doctor and finding a way to combine her love of science with her desire to help others. During her medical studies, she traveled to Cuba, Kenya, and Thailand, providing healthcare to people in need. Mae saw no contradiction between exploring the vastness of space and dedicating herself to improving lives on Earth.

In 1983, a life-changing opportunity presented itself. She learned that NASA was, for the first time, accepting women into the astronaut program. Mae knew this was a chance she couldn't miss. The application process was rigorous, the odds against her astronomical. But she had faced long odds before, and the boundless universe held far more allure than any earthly obstacle.

Out of over 2,000 applicants, Mae Jemison was one of fifteen selected to join NASA's astronaut corps. The years of relentless study, her diverse skillset, and her unwavering spirit led her to this extraordinary moment. Her training was grueling, pushing both her body and mind to their limits. She learned about spacecraft systems, spacewalk procedures, and the intricate science behind spaceflight. But even amidst the complex calculations and dizzying simulators, she never lost sight of her childhood dream.

Finally, in 1992, Mae Jemison made history. Aboard the space shuttle Endeavour, she blasted into orbit, becoming the first African American woman to travel into space. During her eight-day mission, she served as a mission specialist, conducting experiments and making observations that would further our knowledge of both space and the human body's response to its unique environment.

From Earth, young girls of all backgrounds watched Mae Jemison in awe, seeing their own dreams reflected back at them from the depths of space. She was a tangible reminder that a place amongst the stars was theirs for the claiming, regardless of skin color or gender.

Looking down at our planet from orbit, the earthly divisions seemed small. To Mae, the most important mission was fostering a sense of shared responsibility for our fragile world and inspiring a generation of explorers to reach for the impossible.

Mae Jemison's journey didn't end with her return to Earth. After leaving NASA in 1993, she remained a trailblazer and an outspoken advocate for science education and the importance of diversity in STEM fields. She founded an international science camp for students and started the Dorothy Jemison Foundation for Excellence, named in honor of her mother.

Mae's influence spreads far beyond the classroom. She has appeared on television and in films, even playing a role in a Star Trek episode - a beautiful nod to the fictional character who once helped ignite her own passion for space.

Mae Jemison's story is one of boundless ambition met with unrelenting determination. She is a scientist, an explorer, a doctor, a dancer, and a constant reminder that the most important limitations are the ones we set for ourselves. Her footprints, both on Earth and etched amongst the stars, serve as an enduring guide for the generations to come. Because when we dare to dream the impossible, we change not only our own lives, but the boundaries of what we believe is possible for all humankind.

Amidst the lush landscapes and timeworn temples of China, a young scientist named Tu Youyou embarked on a quest unlike any other. Her goal wasn't to unearth hidden treasures or decode forgotten scrolls, but to combat a devastating force - a tiny, yet formidable enemy known as malaria.

Tu Youyou, the Malaria Maverick

Tu Youyou was born in 1930 in the picturesque port city of Ningbo, China. From an early age, she displayed an inquisitive mind and a deep love for the natural world. Her father, a scholar of traditional Chinese medicine, nurtured her curiosity, encouraging her to study the delicate interplay between plants, animals, and human health.

China, an ancient land brimming with rich history and tradition, was also a land plagued by disease. Malaria, a parasitic disease spread by mosquitoes, was a particularly vicious foe. Its symptoms - fevers, chills, and in severe cases, organ damage and death - cast a long shadow over countless lives. Western medicine offered some treatments, like quinine, but these were often expensive, had harsh side effects, and were becoming less reliable as the malaria parasite developed resistance.

Tu Youyou was determined to find a solution, a way to battle this relentless illness. She studied pharmacology, the science of medicines, at Beijing Medical University, immersing herself in the complex world of chemical compounds and their effects on the human body. But Tu

Youyou knew that sometimes, the most potent answers might lie hidden not within a modern laboratory, but within the wisdom passed down through generations.

In 1967, in the midst of China's Cultural Revolution, a turning point came. Chairman Mao Zedong launched a secret military project, known as Project 523, with a specific goal: to find a cure for malaria, which was ravaging North Vietnamese soldiers fighting in the Vietnam War. Tu Youyou, with her expertise in both traditional Chinese medicine and modern pharmacology, was appointed to lead a research team.

The task before her was daunting. Thousands of years of Chinese medical texts existed, filled with potential remedies. Where would one even begin to search? Tu and her team embarked on a meticulous mission, traveling across China and collecting ancient medical manuals. They delved into folk remedies, remedies whispered down through generations, remedies recorded in crumbling scrolls that documented centuries of a battle against disease.

They interviewed practitioners of traditional medicine, seeking out knowledge that had endured the test of time. But simply gathering information was not enough. The true test would lie in the rigorous process of scientific investigation. Could any of these ancient remedies truly work against a disease as persistent as malaria?

Amidst the vast collection of texts, one particular plant caught the team's attention: sweet wormwood (Artemisia annua). This plant had been used in Chinese medicine for centuries to treat fevers - a potential clue to its possible effectiveness against malaria. Tu Youyou and her team painstakingly isolated and extracted the active compound within the plant, a substance named artemisinin.

The initial results were frustrating. The artemisinin compound didn't seem consistently effective against malaria in their early experiments. But Tu Youyou refused to give up. She returned to the ancient texts, searching for any insight that might explain the inconsistency.

Her persistence paid off. A 1,600-year-old text offered a crucial revelation. The ancient instructions detailed preparing sweet wormwood not with boiling water, which could damage the active ingredient, but with a cool extraction process. Adjusting their methods, Tu and her team achieved a breakthrough. The newly extracted artemisinin proved incredibly potent against malaria parasites in animal studies.

The next, most crucial step was testing the treatment on human patients. In a courageous act that reflected her unwavering dedication, Tu Youyou volunteered to be the first person to test the new drug. Understanding the risk, she was confident in the meticulous work her team had done. Thankfully, the human trials were successful, proving that artemisinin was not only effective but safe for use in patients.

Tu Youyou's discovery was a testament to the power of combining ancient wisdom with modern scientific rigor. Instead of dismissing traditional medicine, she sought the diamonds of knowledge that might be hidden within. Her work led to the development of highly effective anti-malarial medications, revolutionizing treatment and saving countless lives across the globe, especially in developing countries.

In 2015, Tu Youyou received the Nobel Prize in Medicine, becoming the first Chinese woman to be удостоled with this prestigious honor. Her recognition was long overdue, and some argued the prize should have been shared with other scientists who'd further refined artemisinin-based therapies. But Tu Youyou's initial discovery, driven by her tenacity and respect for the knowledge of the past, was the undeniable foundation upon which these life-saving treatments were built.

Though fame followed, Tu Youyou remained focused on her work, continuing her research at the China Academy of Traditional Chinese Medicine. When asked about the Nobel Prize, she kept her response humble, characteristic of a woman whose primary motivation was to ease the burden of disease on humanity.

Tu Youyou's story teaches us the importance of looking for solutions in unexpected places. It reminds us that even the oldest texts might hold clues to modern problems, and that respect for diverse knowledge systems is crucial in scientific advancement. Beyond her groundbreaking discovery, Tu Youyou is a role model for scientists everywhere. She showed the world that great achievements are possible through a blend of meticulous study, an open mind, and the relentless determination to find answers that can truly change lives.

Sylvia Earle, The Mermaid Scientist

With a heart full of wonder and boundless determination, Sylvia Earle dared to venture where few had gone before - the very depths of our ocean world. She was a scientist, an explorer, a fearless champion of the blue realm that covers most of our planet. Nicknamed "Her Deepness," Sylvia didn't just study the ocean; she loved it, fought for it, and became one of its most eloquent voices.

Sylvia's love affair with the sea began on the sandy shores of Florida. Born in 1935, she spent countless childhood hours exploring beaches, peering into tide pools, and marveling at the creatures that thrived just beneath the waves. Her family eventually moved to a farm inland, but her young heart forever belonged to the ocean.

Her parents encouraged Sylvia's inquisitive nature. Unlike many girls of her generation, she wasn't pushed towards dolls and dresses, but microscopes and field trips. Her insatiable curiosity extended to all aspects of the natural world. She had a collection of insects, experimented with plants, and wasn't afraid to get her hands dirty in the pursuit of discovery.

As a teenager, Sylvia finally had the chance to experience the ocean not just from the shore, but from within. With borrowed scuba gear, she took her first breaths underwater - a moment that would ignite a lifelong passion for marine life and its preservation.

Sylvia's pursuit of knowledge led her to Florida State University, where she excelled in botany, the study of plants. Yet, the ocean's call remained irresistible. She continued her marine studies, becoming one of the first women to use SCUBA gear for research. This opened a whole new dimension to her explorations. No longer confined to the water's surface, Sylvia could move like a fish amongst the vibrant coral reefs and kelp forests, getting to know the ocean's creatures in ways few had dared before.

In 1964, Sylvia joined an expedition to the Indian Ocean. Though there were other scientists aboard, she was the only woman, a fact that did little to deter her. She dove fearlessly with sharks, conducted research, and continued expanding the boundaries of underwater exploration for women in marine science.

In 1970, Sylvia Earle led the first all-female team of aquanauts in the Tektite II project. Living and working within an underwater laboratory for two weeks, they proved that women could play a vital role in the most ambitious oceanographic endeavors. This mission garnered Sylvia both national recognition and the opportunity to push the limits ever further.

Throughout the 1970s and 1980s, she embarked on daring dives around the world. Using a special suit called the JIM suit, Sylvia walked the ocean floor at depths of over 1,200 feet, setting records and expanding our understanding of the ocean's twilight depths where sunlight barely reaches. She founded two marine engineering companies, continuing to develop innovative technologies that would allow humans to safely explore our underwater world.

Through her expeditions, Sylvia became more than just an observer of the marine environment; she became its advocate. She witnessed firsthand the devastating impacts of pollution, overfishing, and habitat destruction. Ever the scientist, she collected meticulous data and observations, but her mission went far beyond the pursuit of facts. Determined to share the beauty and importance of the ocean with the world, she began writing books, giving lectures, and appearing in documentaries. Her voice was both passionate and informed, her warnings about the threats facing the ocean backed by rigorous research.

In 1990, Sylvia Earle was appointed the first female Chief Scientist of the National Oceanic and Atmospheric Administration (NOAA). It was a position of influence, allowing her to promote a greater awareness of ocean issues on a national level. While the role was a groundbreaking accomplishment, she didn't let titles define her, always returning to her true love: exploration.

Sylvia continued to dive and research, but her focus shifted towards mobilizing others to champion the health of our planet's blue heart. She founded Mission Blue, an organization dedicated to creating "Hope Spots," special marine protected areas around the world that are essential for the health of the ocean.

Sylvia Earle's work reminds us that the ocean isn't simply a beautiful backdrop to our lives; it's essential to the health of the entire planet. The ocean provides us with food, regulates our climate, and is home to a dizzying array of life, much of which remains undiscovered. Yet, this vital ecosystem is under unprecedented threat.

Sylvia, now in her eighties, continues to be a tireless voice for the ocean, her spirit undimmed and her sense of urgency greater than ever. She uses underwater technology to bring the ocean's beauty and wonder into classrooms, inspiring young people with the endless potential for discovery and the undeniable need to protect this watery realm that gives us life.

Sylvia Earle, through her remarkable explorations, advocacy, and unwavering love for the sea, has earned her place as an icon of ocean conservation. She teaches us that even one person with a passion, a voice, and the courage to explore can make a lasting impact on our world and the generations to come.

Hedy Lamarr, The Movie Star Inventor

Beneath the dazzling lights and glamorous image of one of Hollywood's most celebrated stars lived a brilliant mind brimming with ideas that would change the world. Hedy Lamarr was far more than just a beautiful face; she was an inventor whose ingenious creation helped shape the modern technologies we rely on every day.

Hedy's tale begins in Austria in 1914, where she was born Hedwig Kiesler. Her father, a successful banker, sparked her early curiosity. He would explain the workings of machines and encourage her to ask questions. Her mother, a concert pianist, instilled in her an artistic spirit and appreciation for beauty. Hedy was a brilliant child, her mind as dazzling as her looks.

Acting became her first passion, and as a teenager, she began a successful career in European films. It was her captivating role in the controversial Czech film "Ecstasy" that brought her to the attention of Hollywood mogul Louis B. Mayer. Sensing both her star power and her vulnerabilities, he persuaded her to change her name, offering the allure and mystique of Hedy Lamarr.

Hollywood in the Golden Age was synonymous with glamour - beautiful stars, extravagant costumes, and fantastical storylines. While Hedy quickly ascended to stardom, known for her striking beauty and undeniable screen presence, she felt restless. The parties, the premieres, and the endless studio publicity didn't satisfy her thirst for knowledge or her desire to be challenged.

Seeking an outlet for her restless intellect, she turned to invention. With characteristic determination, she set up an inventing space in her home, complete with drafting tables and all the tools she'd need. Even after grueling days on set, she sought refuge in her workshop, tinkering with ideas and immersing herself in the world of problem-solving.

Her first patented invention was a practical one, inspired by the challenges she observed on bustling film sets. She designed an improved traffic light, aiming to ease congestion and improve safety on busy streets. Though the world wasn't yet ready for her idea, the experience demonstrated her ability to think creatively and identify ways to improve everyday life through invention.

World War II had begun, casting a dark shadow over Europe and eventually drawing the United States into its grip. Hedy, haunted by the horrors happening in her homeland and the dangers threatening democracy, felt compelled to do her part. Her acting skills she knew could bolster morale, and she used her celebrity status in wartime rallies, encouraging people to support the war effort. But she longed to make a more significant, more direct contribution.

It was through her friendship with the avant-garde composer George Antheil that an ingenious idea began to take shape. They both shared a deep concern over the war and a fascination with technology. Antheil had experimented with automated musical instruments and had dabbled in ways to control torpedoes remotely using radio signals, which could be easily jammed by the enemy.

Drawing on her knowledge of weapons systems and Antheil's experience in musical synchronization, Hedy devised a game-changing solution. What if instead of a single radio frequency, they used a system of rapidly switching frequencies to guide torpedoes - a "frequency hopping" method that would be nearly impossible for the enemy to disrupt?

Hedy and George patented their frequency-hopping spread spectrum technology in 1942. Confident in the importance of their invention, they presented it to the U.S. Navy. However, they were met with disbelief and skepticism. Technology was viewed as a strictly male domain, and the idea that a glamorous movie star could also be a brilliant inventor simply went over the heads of military officials. Sadly, their visionary idea was dismissed and filed away, its true potential unrecognized.

Despite this disappointing setback, Hedy continued to invent, finding joy in the act of creation and problem-solving. Yet, the missed opportunity of her war-time invention would linger, a bittersweet reminder of "what could have been". It would take decades for the world to appreciate the brilliance of her idea.

As the war ended, Hedy continued her Hollywood career, starring in numerous successful films. But her legacy was only just beginning to be written. In the 1950s, technology began to catch up with Hedy Lamarr's vision. Her frequency-hopping concept proved vital, though she received neither credit nor compensation at the time. Her invention became the foundation for secure military communications, and later enabled a stunning array of wireless technologies we take for granted today – Bluetooth, GPS, and WiFi systems all owe their existence to her ingenious solution.

It wasn't until the 1990s, as her Hollywood career faded, that recognition for her scientific contributions finally came. Awards and honors began to replace movie scripts, shining a long-overdue spotlight on her brilliant, inventive mind.

Hedy Lamarr passed away in 2000, leaving a complex and inspiring legacy. She proved to the world that beauty and brains are not mutually exclusive, that a passion for invention and scientific discovery can exist alongside artistic expression and fame. She shattered stereotypes and paved the way for other women who dared to venture into the traditionally male-dominated world of science and technology.

Hedy Lamarr's story offers a powerful lesson: Never underestimate someone based on their appearance or career path. Extraordinary ideas can come from the most unexpected places. And while recognition delayed is better than never, society must work harder to uplift and support brilliant women like her, giving their ideas the respect and consideration they deserve the moment they are presented.

Grace Hopper, The Code Whisperer

In a world dominated by hulking machines and cryptic strings of numbers, Grace Hopper saw a future where computers would become more accessible, more user-friendly, and ultimately transform every aspect of human life. With a razor-sharp intellect and a playful spirit, she became a pioneer of computer programming, earning the nickname "Amazing Grace" for her groundbreaking work.

Grace's journey began in 1906 in the bustling metropolis of New York City. From a young age, she possessed a relentless curiosity, not content with simply accepting how things worked, but driven to dissect them and understand their inner workings. Grace took apart alarm clocks, put them back together (mostly), and showed a remarkable aptitude for mathematics, an inheritance perhaps from her grandfather, a renowned mathematician.

Her parents encouraged Grace's inquisitive nature, providing her with opportunities that were unusual for a girl of her era. She attended Vassar College, excelling in mathematics and physics, then went on to earn her master's degree and a Ph.D. in mathematics from Yale University - rare accomplishments for a woman at the time. Grace seemed destined for a life in academia, teaching and pushing the boundaries of mathematical knowledge. But the outbreak of World War II changed the trajectory of her life.

Eager to do her part for the war effort, Grace left the hallowed halls of university to join the Navy Reserves. She was determined to contribute, even though mathematics might seem far removed from the battlefields. But fate, and her unique skill set, had a different plan in store.

Grace was assigned to the Bureau of Ordnance Computation Project at Harvard University. Here, she found herself face-to-face with an electromechanical beast the Mark I computer. It was a behemoth of a machine, a whirlwind of clicking relays and whirring switches, filling an entire room. Its purpose? To perform rapid ballistic calculations, crucial for the war effort. Grace Hopper was about to learn the language of computers, becoming one of the first programmers on this groundbreaking machine.

Undeterred by the Mark I's complexity, Grace dove into the task with characteristic enthusiasm and determination.

She studied its intricate workings, its myriad switches and connections, grasping that this complex machine operated on the fundamental principles of logic and mathematics she knew so well.

Programming the Mark I didn't involve the sleek computer languages we use today. It meant physically manipulating switches, plugging and unplugging wires, and feeding the machine instructions on punch cards. It was a painstaking and often frustrating process, but Grace saw beyond the cumbersome mechanics, understanding the immense potential these machines held.

Working on the war effort, Grace quickly realized that a major obstacle prevented the wider adoption and usefulness of computers: they were incredibly difficult to speak to. Programmers relied on numerical codes, a language far removed from the way humans naturally think and communicate. Grace believed there had to be a better way.

She envisioned a future where one could instruct a computer using plain English words, revolutionizing its accessibility beyond the small circle of highly-trained engineers and mathematicians. This was a radical idea for its time, and many dismissed it as impossible. But

Grace Hopper was never one to shy away from a challenge.

While working on the successor to the Mark I, the Mark II, Grace made a frustrating discovery. A moth had flown into a relay and was causing errors in the machine, the origin of the modern-day computer "bug." While removing the moth was relatively simple, the incident solidified in her mind the importance of creating computers less prone to errors and easier to debug.

With unwavering determination, Grace began developing a new programming language. Instead of obscure numerical codes, it would use English-like commands, making it vastly easier for people to communicate with computers. This new language, called FLOW-MATIC, became the precursor to COBOL, one of the earliest and most widely used high-level programming languages, driving the growth of the software industry.

Grace Hopper's work didn't stop there. Throughout her long and illustrious career, she advocated tirelessly for making computers more user-friendly. She urged the Navy to transition from paper manuals to computer-accessible documentation. She developed standards for testing computer systems and programming languages, ensuring reliability - an important consideration as computers began to impact critical industries beyond military calculations.

Though Grace retired from the Navy in 1986, at the age of 80, she was far from finished with her mission. She continued lecturing, consulting, and teaching, working to bridge the gap between humans and computers. With her signature wit and engaging style, she inspired countless young people to explore the world of computers and understand the power they held.

Her playful spirit shone brightly, a stark contrast to the stereotype of the stoic programmer. When someone asked her why the speed of light was only 186,000 miles per second, she would cut off a piece of wire - about a foot long- and explain that it represented a nanosecond, the amount of time it takes light to travel that distance. She carried these nanosecond reminders of the finite limitations technology faced - a constant grounding even amidst her boundless optimism for the future.

Grace Hopper passed away in 1992, leaving behind an enduring legacy in the realm of computer science. She is remembered not only for her technical brilliance but for championing simplicity and user-friendliness - qualities that transformed computers from specialized tools into the ubiquitous technology we rely on today. Perhaps her greatest achievement, however, was in paving the way for countless individuals, regardless of gender or background, to embrace the power of computers and to shape the future through code.

Katherine Johnson, The Rocket Mathematician

Hidden amongst the vast complex at NASA, amidst the roar of rocket engines and the hushed calculations of engineers, Katherine Johnson made history. Armed with a brilliant mind, unshakeable determination, and a love for numbers, she defied the barriers of both race and gender, becoming an indispensable part of America's historic journey into space.

Katherine's story begins in West Virginia in 1918. From an early age, she displayed an extraordinary aptitude for mathematics. She loved to count, finding numbers in everything - steps on the stairway, dishes on the table, and stars in the night sky. Katherine was determined to learn everything she could, and her parents, recognizing her potential, made great sacrifices to ensure she received the best education possible despite the limitations imposed by segregation.

Her brilliance shone brightly. Katherine skipped multiple grades, entered high school at the age of ten, and then went on to West Virginia State College, a historically Black institution. There, her professors, especially the mathematician W. W. Schieffelin Claytor, quickly recognized her as a remarkable talent. He created new courses specifically for Katherine, pushing her to reach her full potential. She graduated summa cum laude in 1937, with degrees in both mathematics and French.

Though Katherine initially became a school teacher, the path her life would take shifted dramatically when an opportunity arose in 1953. Through a family connection, she learned that the Langley Memorial Aeronautical Laboratory, part of the National Advisory Committee for Aeronautics (NACA), was seeking African American women talented in mathematics. Despite segregation, the push to develop technologies to gain an edge over the Soviet Union in the aerospace race created a small opening. Katherine jumped at the chance.

At Langley, Katherine joined the West Area Computers, a group of African American women mathematicians who performed complex calculations by hand. These women, known as "human computers," were vital to the aeronautical research at NACA before electronic computers became widespread. While vital to the work at NACA, their contributions were often undervalued due to both gender and racial biases.

Katherine, however, was not one to remain in the shadows. Her brilliance and hard work quickly set her apart. In a matter of weeks, she was assigned to the prestigious Flight Research Division, where her mathematical skills became indispensable in understanding the complexities of aircraft trajectories and control problems.

As the 1960s began, the world was caught in the space race, and NACA transformed into its successor, NASA. Katherine became an integral part of this historic endeavor, her calculations laying the foundation for the success of missions that would redefine our understanding of humankind's place in the universe.

One of her most important contributions was calculating the trajectory for Alan Shepard's 1961 flight, making him the first American in space. Her work ensured his safe launch and his even more critical return back to Earth. Yet, initially, like so many of the women 'computers,' her contributions remained largely unacknowledged.

Katherine's most iconic moment came during the lead-up to John Glenn's historic 1962 orbital flight. While new electronic computers had been introduced, Glenn didn't entirely trust the machines. He specifically requested that

Katherine Johnson double-check the calculations for his trajectory - calculations that would determine whether he would safely orbit the Earth and return home. It was a testament to his faith in a Black woman mathematician's skills in a segregated workspace, and his faith was rewarded. Her calculations proved correct, and John Glenn's mission was a resounding success.

Throughout her trailblazing career at NASA, Katherine Johnson authored or co-authored numerous research reports, her brilliance instrumental in the successes of Project Mercury, the Apollo moon missions, and early development of the Space Shuttle program. Yet, her name remained largely unknown outside of NASA.

Katherine, with quiet dignity, focused on the work itself, driven by more than the quest for recognition. She possessed a deep love for the elegance of numbers and the profound challenges that spaceflight presented. She tackled each mathematical equation with determination and precision, knowing that lives depended on her accuracy.

It wasn't until years into retirement that Katherine Johnson's remarkable story gained widespread recognition. The 2016 book "Hidden Figures" and its subsequent film adaptation shone a long-overdue spotlight on the vital contributions of her and the other African American women mathematicians at Langley. Finally, the world saw her for what she truly was: a pioneer who broke down barriers and played a crucial role in one of humanity's greatest achievements.

Katherine Johnson's legacy extends far beyond her calculations. She became a symbol for overcoming societal barriers, proving that brilliance and determination transcend race and gender. She tirelessly encouraged young people, especially girls, to pursue education in STEM fields, paving the way for a more diverse and inclusive scientific community.

Katherine Johnson passed away in 2020 at the age of 101. She is remembered as a brilliant mathematician, a trailblazer, and a woman whose story tells us that the most powerful forces shaping the universe of innovation lie in the boundless potential of the human mind.

Rosalind Franklin, The Photo that Changed the World

In the realm of science, true greatness is found not only in groundbreaking discoveries, but in the pursuit of knowledge itself, even when recognition might be fleeting. Rosalind Franklin was a brilliant scientist whose meticulous work was key to unlocking the secrets of DNA - the very building blocks of life. Yet, for far too long, her contributions were obscured, a casualty of both the male-dominated scientific landscape of her time and her own untimely passing.

Rosalind's story began in London, 1920. Born into a world on the brink of social and technological upheaval, she was not content with the expectations society placed upon girls of her generation. From a young age, she possessed a fierce intellect and an unwavering curiosity about how the world worked. With the support of her family, Rosalind excelled in school, particularly in science and mathematics.

She attended Cambridge University, where she broadened her scientific understanding and found her calling in the study of physical chemistry. World War II cast a shadow over her time as a student, and her research on the properties of coal would later prove to be crucial for the war effort, providing insight into the creation of more effective gas masks.

Upon graduating, Rosalind's journey led her to Paris, where she honed her skills in the cutting-edge technique of X-ray crystallography. This technique involved shooting X-rays at a crystallized sample of a molecule. The pattern created by the diffracting X-rays could be analyzed to reveal the molecule's intricate three-dimensional structure. Rosalind's meticulous work and deep understanding of X-ray analysis set her apart as an expert in the field.

In 1951, opportunity brought Rosalind back to London, to King's College. She was invited to join a team tasked with understanding the structure of DNA. The field was abuzz with excitement, as scientists knew this molecule was somehow the key to heredity, but its precise structure and function remained a mystery.

Rosalind set to work with unwavering dedication and exceptional skill. Using her expertise in X-ray crystallography, she painstakingly prepared purified samples of DNA and captured images of astounding brilliance. One, in particular, became known as Photo 51.

It displayed a clear X-shaped pattern, hinting at the double helix structure of DNA, a piece of the puzzle that would change our understanding of life forever.

However, navigating a male-dominated research environment was fraught with difficulties. Rosalind's personality, described as direct and at times even confrontational, clashed with colleagues like Maurice Wilkins. This strained professional relationship, combined with a misunderstanding about her role in the lab, created an atmosphere where collaboration became increasingly difficult.

During this time, James Watson and Francis Crick, scientists at Cambridge University, were also hot on the trail of DNA's structure. Through a series of events still debated by historians, they gained access to Rosalind's Photo 51 without her knowledge. This image, along with some of her other unpublished data, proved vital in their own model building. Watson and Crick, with the crucial insights gleaned from Rosalind's work, went on to publish the groundbreaking double helix model of DNA in 1953.

Tragically, Rosalind was never fully aware of the role her meticulous work played in their historic discovery. Having left King's College due to the unpleasant atmosphere, she excelled in other fields. She conducted pioneering research on the structure of viruses, work that paved the way for modern virology.

However, Rosalind's brilliant career was cut short. She passed away from ovarian cancer in 1958, at the young age of 37. Her death was a profound loss to the scientific community. Sadly, the Nobel Prize, the highest recognition for scientific achievement, isn't awarded posthumously.

Four years after her death, in 1962, Watson, Crick, and Wilkins were awarded the Nobel Prize in Medicine for their DNA discovery. Rosalind Franklin's name was barely a footnote in their acceptance speeches. While there is debate on whether she would have shared the Nobel had she lived, the lack of public acknowledgement of her substantial contribution was an injustice.

It took decades for the full importance of Rosalind Franklin's work to become widely recognized. As the scientific community gained a better understanding of the true events surrounding the discovery of DNA's structure, her brilliance became undeniable. Biographers and historians helped to reshape the narrative, bringing her story out of the shadows.

Today, Rosalind Franklin is celebrated as a scientific pioneer. Her Photo 51 is hailed as a masterpiece of scientific imaging, a vital key to unlocking the secrets of life itself. She is an undeniable role model to young scientists everywhere, especially women, who are inspired by her pursuit of knowledge in the face of prejudice and a tragically shortened career.

Though robbed of her due recognition throughout much of her life, Rosalind Franklin's legacy stands the test of time. Her story teaches us that true scientific progress relies on collaboration, respect, and the acknowledgement that extraordinary discoveries can come from the most unexpected places. Most importantly, it reminds us that even when fame and recognition are delayed, the tireless pursuit of knowledge creates ripples that endure through history

Elizabeth Blackwell, The Brave Doctor

At a time when the very idea of a female doctor was considered ludicrous, Elizabeth Blackwell defied societal norms and shattered the glass ceiling of the medical profession. Through unwavering determination and an unshakeable belief in her capabilities, she became the first woman to earn a medical degree in the United States and a champion for women's health and education.

Elizabeth's remarkable journey began in Bristol, England, in 1821. Hers was a large, lively household where intellectual curiosity and social reform were encouraged. Yet, family stability would prove elusive. A fire destroyed her father's sugar refinery, forcing them to pursue opportunities in America. The family settled in New York City, and there, young Elizabeth witnessed firsthand the stark inequalities, poverty, and social injustices that prevailed in the burgeoning metropolis.

Tragedy struck when her beloved father passed away, leaving the Blackwell family without a primary source of income. To help support her mother and siblings, Elizabeth, along with her sisters, opened a school.

Teaching became her first profession, but she yearned for a path that would allow her to make more of a direct impact on people's lives.

Her path in life took an unexpected turn when a dear friend fell gravely ill. On her deathbed, the friend lamented that her suffering would have been lessened had she been attended by a female physician. These words resonated deeply with Elizabeth. The idea of a woman as a doctor, at the time, seemed completely radical, but it sparked something within her - a sense of purpose and a determination to challenge the status quo.

The path to becoming a doctor would be an uphill battle. Medical schools in the 1840s simply did not accept women. Elizabeth sent applications far and wide, only to be met with rejection after rejection. Many of the denial letters were insulting, questioning her intellect and her sanity for pursuing such an outlandish ambition.

However, Elizabeth Blackwell was not one to surrender in the face of adversity. In a stroke of near-miraculous luck, she received an acceptance letter from Geneva Medical College in rural New York. But the acceptance turned out to be a mix-up. The male faculty, assuming her application to be a joke, had put the decision of whether to admit a woman to a student vote. The young men, thinking it a harmless prank, voted yes.

Undeterred by the less than ideal circumstances of her acceptance, Elizabeth saw it as an opportunity to prove herself. When she arrived in Geneva in 1847, she was met with a mixture of astonishment, skepticism, and even hostility. Many locals assumed she was a woman of loose morals; the concept of a woman pursuing the 'masculine' profession of medicine was simply so far outside societal norms that it didn't compute in the minds of many.

Elizabeth, ever determined, rose above the prejudice. She studied relentlessly, demonstrating her exceptional intellect and dedication to her patients. Slowly, through hard work and determination, she began to earn the respect, however grudging, of some of her classmates and professors.

Elizabeth's presence at the medical school was transformative. She challenged the prevailing attitudes of the time, forcing her male colleagues to confront their own preconceived notions about women's capabilities. Her journey also highlighted the need for proper care for women patients, many of whom felt uncomfortable being examined by male doctors and were therefore reluctant to seek crucial medical attention.

In 1849, Elizabeth Blackwell made history, graduating at the top of her class as the first woman to earn a medical degree in the United States. Her achievement was widely reported, with reactions ranging from praise to mockery. But Elizabeth had proven, beyond a shadow of a doubt, that women were just as capable as men when it came to the rigorous study and practice of medicine.

Determined to further her medical training, Elizabeth traveled to Europe where there was slightly greater acceptance of female physicians. She studied in hospitals in both Paris and London, expanding her knowledge of midwifery and gaining valuable practical experience. However, a horrible accident would once again change the course of her life. While treating an infant with a contagious eye infection, she contracted the disease herself, resulting in the loss of sight in one eye. Her dreams of becoming a surgeon were dashed.

Undeterred, Elizabeth returned to New York City in 1851. The doors of established hospitals remained closed to her as a woman, so, with her characteristic resolve, she opened her own small clinic. Initially, patients were few and often treated her with disdain, but her reputation for skill and unwavering compassion gradually grew. Her clinic focused on providing care for poor women and children, addressing a desperate need in the city's crowded and underserved neighborhoods.

In 1857, Elizabeth, along with her sister Emily (who had followed in her footsteps and also become a doctor) and another female physician, Marie Zakrzewska, expanded their clinic into the New York Infirmary for Indigent Women and Children. This institution was groundbreaking, not only providing medical care to those in need, but also being entirely run by women.

Recognizing the dire need to open pathways for other women to enter the medical profession, Elizabeth Blackwell founded the Women's Medical College of the New York Infirmary in 1868. It served as one of the first medical schools in the country dedicated to training women to become doctors, ensuring that her legacy would extend far beyond her own practice.

Throughout her life, Elizabeth Blackwell was a tireless advocate for women's health issues, public hygiene, and medical education reforms. She wrote and lectured extensively, her voice challenging the medical norms of the time. But her influence extended beyond medicine.

She was a strong believer in women's suffrage and actively challenged the societal barriers that confined women to the domestic realm.

Elizabeth Blackwell never married or had children of her own, dedicating her life entirely to her mission of healing and empowering others. She lived to the age of 89, passing away in England in 1910. By then, the landscape of medicine had vastly changed. Women attending medical school was no longer an absurdity, but rather an enduring reality, thanks in large part to her courage and the path she forged.

Elizabeth Blackwell's legacy lies not only in her own achievements, but in the countless women physicians following in her footsteps. Her story reminds us that breaking down the walls of prejudice requires unwavering determination, a commitment to excellence, and the belief that creating a more just and equitable world is a goal always worth pursuing.

Chien-Shiung Wu, The Queen of the Experiment

In the realm of physics, where scientists grappled with the fundamental forces of the universe, Chien-Shiung Wu carved a path that shattered expectations and overturned long-held scientific principles. Meticulous in her experimentation and fearless in questioning conventional wisdom, she earned the rightful moniker "The First Lady of Physics." Yet, her achievements were sadly overlooked when the prestige of the Nobel Prize was bestowed.

Chien-Shiung Wu's story began in 1912 in a small town near Shanghai, China. A time of change was bubbling in China, with growing movements advocating for women's rights and increased access to education. Her parents were at the forefront of this change. Her father, an ardent believer in equality, founded an elementary school dedicated to providing girls with the same opportunities for learning as boys. It was in this nurturing environment that Chien-Shiung's curious mind blossomed.

Showing a prodigious aptitude for science and mathematics, Chien-Shiung excelled in school. Her path, though smoother than most girls in China at the time, was not without obstacles. To pursue higher education, she would have to travel far from home, defying social expectations. However, Chien-Shiung was undeterred, motivated by an insatiable thirst for knowledge that pushed her beyond the confines of her small town.

In 1934, Chien-Shiung graduated with top honors from National Central University in Nanjing. Eager to continue her scientific exploration, her next step was a daring one. She set sail for the United States, embarking on a journey that would change the course of her life and our understanding of physics.

Arriving in San Francisco, she was faced with the harsh realities of prejudice and the sexism prevalent in the scientific community. Despite her brilliance, many American universities were hesitant to admit a female student, especially one of foreign origin. Thankfully, her academic record spoke for itself. She earned a place at the University of California, Berkeley, a hub of cutting-edge physics research. There, Chien-Shiung's exceptional abilities came to the forefront. She immersed herself in the study of nuclear physics, drawn to the complexities of the invisible world of atoms and particles.

Upon completing her doctorate in 1940, Chien-Shiung continued her research career during a time when opportunities for women scientists were still severely limited. Yet her dedication and expertise were undeniable. She landed teaching positions at prestigious East Coast institutions, including Smith College and Princeton University. Eventually, she joined the faculty at Columbia University, where she would make her most groundbreaking discoveries.

World War II had cast its shadow over the field of physics, with research primarily focused on the race to build a nuclear weapon. Chien-Shiung's own expertise in nuclear processes put her in high demand. She joined the Manhattan Project, contributing to the development of processes for uranium enrichment. Though pivotal to the war effort, this collaboration would later bring a sense of regret, as she witnessed the devastation wrought by the very power she helped to weaponize.

Chien-Shiung's most famous work focused on a fundamental principle in physics called the conservation of parity. This principle held that the universe, when mirrored, should behave identically. In other words, if you could duplicate a physical process exactly, but with everything reversed (left becoming right and vice versa), the mirrored experiment should produce the same results. While this seems like an intuitive concept, in the realm of particle physics, nature doesn't always follow common sense.

In the 1950s, two theoretical physicists, Tsung-Dao Lee and Chen-Ning Yang, wondered if parity conservation held true at the subatomic level in a type of nuclear decay called beta decay. Realizing that this could be tested experimentally, they reached out to the brilliant experimentalist Chien-Shiung Wu. Always eager to challenge convention, she meticulously designed an experiment to answer their daring question.

Wu's experiment was a masterpiece of precision and ingenuity. She cooled cobalt-60 atoms, aligning their nuclear spins, to near absolute zero. She then meticulously monitored how they underwent beta decay. The results were astounding. The decay process did not perfectly mirror itself! Particles were preferentially emitted in a specific direction, violating parity conservation, a result that shocked the physics world.

Lee and Yang's theoretical prediction, confirmed by Wu's irrefutable experimental data, changed our understanding of fundamental forces. It was a testament to Wu's exceptional ability to translate abstract theoretical concepts into testable experiments that drove the discovery forward.

In 1957, Lee and Yang were awarded the Nobel Prize in Physics for their theoretical work. Sadly, Chien-Shiung Wu's indispensable contribution was overlooked. This omission was a glaring injustice, reflecting the deep-seated biases that continued to hinder recognition of women scientists, despite clear evidence of their brilliance.

Undeterred, Wu continued her groundbreaking research. She became the first woman to be elected president of the American Physical Society, and received countless belated honors, including the prestigious Wolf Prize in Physics in 1978. Yet, the sting of the missed Nobel Prize, a testament to both societal prejudice and oversight, would remain with her.

Chien-Shiung Wu dedicated her life to unraveling the secrets held within the atomic nucleus. She conducted investigations on the properties of beta decay, made contributions to our understanding of the sickle cell disease, and became a staunch advocate for educational initiatives, encouraging countless young people, especially girls, to pursue careers in STEM fields.

Chien-Shiung Wu passed away in 1997 at the age of 84, leaving behind an enduring legacy in the realm of physics. While fame and the prestige of a Nobel Prize may have been unjustly denied, her groundbreaking work revolutionized our understanding of the universe. She is an inspiration to anyone, regardless of gender or background, who believes in the power of human curiosity to achieve the extraordinary.

Printed in Great Britain
by Amazon